FALLING FOR FUN
GRAVITY IN ACTION

By Nathan Lepora

**Consultant: Suzy Gazlay, M.A.,
science curriculum resource teacher**

 Gareth Stevens
Publishing

Please visit our web site at www.garethstevens.com.
For a free catalog describing our list of high-quality books, call 1-800-542-2595 (USA)
or 1-800-387-3178 (Canada). Our fax: 1-877-542-2596

Library of Congress Cataloging-in-Publication Data
Lepora, Nathan.
    Falling for fun : gravity in action / Nathan Lepora. — North American ed.
       p. cm. — (The science behind thrill rides)
    Includes index.
    ISBN-10: 0-8368-8944-4   ISBN-13: 978-0-8368-8944-4 (lib. bdg.)
    ISBN-10: 0-8368-8949-5   ISBN-13: 978-0-8368-8949-9 (softcover)
      1. Gravity—Juvenile literature.   2. Force and energy—Juvenile
    literature. I. Title.
    QC178.L39   2008
    531'.14—dc22   2007042001

This North American edition first published in 2008 by
Gareth Stevens Publishing
A Weekly Reader® Company
1 Reader's Digest Road
Pleasantville, NY 10570-7000 USA

This U.S. edition copyright © 2008 by Gareth Stevens, Inc. Original edition copyright © 2007 by ticktock Media Ltd.
First published in Great Britain in 2007 by ticktock Media Ltd., Unit 2, Orchard Business Centre, North Farm Road,
Tunbridge Wells, Kent, TN2 3XF United Kingdom

ticktock Project Editor: Sophie Furse
ticktock Picture Researcher: Lizzie Knowles
ticktock Project Designer: Hayley Terry
With thanks to: Carol Ryback, Hayley Terry, and Suzy Gazlay

Gareth Stevens Editor: Jayne Keedle
Gareth Stevens Creative Director: Lisa Donovan
Gareth Stevens Graphic Designer: Farimah Toosi
Gareth Stevens Cover Designer: Yin Ling Wong

Picture credits (t = top; b = bottom; c = center; l = left; r = right):
Illustrations by Justin Spain
Jeff Greenberg/Science Photo Library: cover. Robb Alvey www.themeparkreview.com: 4, 16c. Adam Bailey/Action Plus:
8. Cedar Point: 25. CJM Photography/Alamy: 17. Kitt Cooper-Smith/Alamy: 10–11 main. Ira Chaplain/Rex Features: 19
inset. Chad Ehlers/Stock Connection/Rex Features: 22–23 main. Andrew Fox/Alamy: 5. Robert Harding Picture Library
Ltd/Alamy: 13. iStockphoto: 14. Noah K. Murray/Star Ledger/Corbis: 20l. M. Timothy O'Keefe: Alamy: 9. Roger
Ressmeyer/Corbis: 12c. Shutterstock: contents page, 6–7, 11 inset, 18, 20–21 background, 21bl, 26–27. Hayley Terry:
10c, 16b. Ticktock Media Archive: 21tl. www.ultimaterollercoaster.com: 15.

Every effort has been made to trace copyright holders, and we apologize in advance for any omissions. We would be
pleased to insert the appropriate acknowledgments in any subsequent edition of this publication.

Printed in the United States of America

1 2 3 4 5 6 7 8 9 10 09 08 07

CONTENTS

CHAPTER 1: GRAVITY

The roller coaster crawls slowly to the top of the first hill. This isn't so bad, you think. Then it hits you. You're perched at the very top and the only place to go is down! Suddenly, you're hurtling to the ground at breathtaking **speed**. Now you're screaming for your life!

WHAT IS GRAVITY?

Gravity pulls roller coaster cars, and everything else, toward Earth. Without the force of gravity, all **matter,** even you, would float off into space. Gravity also causes objects to speed up, as they fall to the ground. Roller coasters could not work without gravity.

Gravity is a constant, one-way force that pulls objects toward the middle of Earth. Imagine digging a hole in the United States and another one in China. If you dropped a ball down each hole, the balls would keep falling until they met each other at the center of Earth!

DROP COASTERS

Want to feel like you're falling to the center of the Earth? Ride a drop coaster! It's the steepest type of roller coaster. A vertical track drops the coaster straight down.

Oblivion at Alton Towers in the United Kingdom was the first drop coaster in the world. The ride plummets into a gaping hole in the ground.

WHAT GOES UP

Everyone knows that what goes up must come down. When a roller coaster car climbs up a hill, you know it has to come whooshing down the other side.

Coaster cars roll along on wheels that are locked onto tracks that twist and turn. The tracks guide the cars through loops and turns. You race downhill, feeling as if you're going to crash into the ground. Then, at the last second, the track takes you back up again.

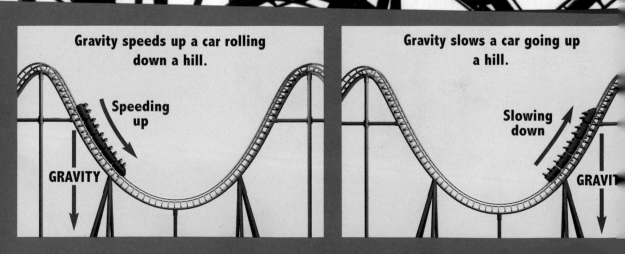

Gravity speeds up a car rolling down a hill.

Speeding up

GRAVITY

Gravity slows a car going up a hill.

Slowing down

GRAVIT

GRAVITY AND ACCELERATION

Gravity makes falling objects fall faster. This change in speed over time is called **acceleration**. As an object moves upward, gravity also pulls down on it. The object slows. That is called **deceleration**.

The speed of a roller coaster is controlled by the slope of the tracks. Going downhill, roller coasters accelerate to faster speeds. The steeper the slope, the faster they go. They slow down when they reach the track's lowest point.

Climbing the next hill, the cars decelerate. As they crawl to the top, you brace yourself for the next thrilling drop!

The speed of a roller coaster ride changes with every hill and dip.

THAT'S AMAZING!

A roller coaster on the Moon would be really boring. The Moon's weak gravity would make the ride very slow.

CHAPTER 2: WEIGHT

You hang on tight as the roller coaster dips and swerves. Sometimes you feel so light, you worry that you'll fly right out of your seat! Other times, you feel as heavy as lead. During the ride, **forces** push on you that make you feel suddenly light or heavy.

WEIGHTY FORCES

When you lift something, you fight against gravity. Your muscles provide the force to lift an object. At the same time, gravity pulls the object back to the floor. That heavy feeling is the pull of gravity on an object's **mass.**

An object's mass is the amount of matter that makes up the object. A stone, for instance, has a greater mass than a sponge. Gravity pulls on an object's mass. That's what gives an object its **weight.**

A weight-lifter struggles against gravity.

DID YOU KNOW?

If the pull of Earth's gravity suddenly halved in strength, the mass of everything would stay the same but everything would weigh half as much.

IMAGINARY WEIGHT

You roar over a hill on a roller coaster. Suddenly, you feel lighter. Swooping through the dip at the bottom of the hill, you feel heavy. Your body mass hasn't changed. So why do you feel as if your weight is changing?

You feel light going over a hill.

THAT'S AMAZING!

Italian mathematician Galileo Galilei (1564–1642) measured how gravity causes acceleration. In one experiment he dropped various sized cannon balls off the Leaning Tower of Pisa. He discovered that different masses fall with the same acceleration.

you accelerate in one direction, you get a feeling of weight in the
posite direction. Speeding up a hill, you feel as if a force is bearing down
you. You are pushed against the seat. The seat stays still as your body
ttens against it. All that fools your brain into thinking you are heavier.

oller coaster accelerating downhill makes you feel lighter. You are lifted
your seat. Your insides seem to float.

You feel heavy going
through a dip.

Every time the roller coaster changes speed or direction, a force pushes against you. The combination of forces acting on your body in a moving roller coaster is called a **g-force.**

G-FORCE

G-force measures the force on your body from acceleration. One g is the normal weight you feel from gravity. In zero g-force, you feel weightless.

Roller coasters can give forces of more than four g. That makes you feel four times heavier than you normally do.

Pilots are trained in special machines (above) so they get used to how g-forces feel.

THAT'S AMAZING!

Fighter plane turns can produce a force of almost ten g. Pilots feel ten times heavier than normal!

BEST COASTER SEATS

Most people think the best seats are at the front of a roller coaster. Those seats give you a great view of the bends and loops as you hurtle toward them.

Some coaster fans prefer the back seats. The back cars accelerate faster over the top of a hill, so riders feel more g-forces!

These thrill-seekers are enjoying the effects of g-forces.

FREE FALL

Did you ever wish you could fly like Superman? For a sky diver, free falling is the next best thing. An object is in **free fall** when acceleration comes only from gravity. In free fall, no other forces are at work.

Normally, you feel the effects of gravity pressing you to the ground. In midair, the only force you feel is gravity. You feel **weightless**. You don't have to jump out of an airplane to find out how that feels. You can experience weightlessness when you ride a roller coaster!

Free fall ends when the parachute opens, slowing the sky diver's descent.

THAT'S AMAZING!

Being weightless may sound like fun but some astronauts get space motion sickness in zero gravity.

AIRTIME

Free fall on a roller coaster is called **airtime.** You feel airtime when the car shoots over a hill or drops straight down.

Superman: The Escape has the longest airtime of any coaster. The ride shoots up forty stories and then drops to Earth. While in free fall you feel weightless for more than six seconds!

Superman: The Escape at Six Flags Magic Mountain, California.

CHAPTER 4: CENTER OF GRAVITY

Not all theme park rides use hills for thrills. Some rides actually fall over! How they fall depends upon where their **center of gravity** is located. This center point is where an object's weight is concentrated.

BALANCING

To stay upright, an object's weight must be balanced. An object's balancing point is it called its center of gravity. For example, you must find the middle point of a ruler to balance it on one finger. Put your finger anywhere else and the ruler will wobble and tip over.

Objects fall over if their center of gravity is unstable. Their center of gravity must be supported in the proper place.

TOPPLE TOWER

El Volador is a Topple Tower at Bellewaerde Theme Park in Belgium. It falls over just when riders least expect it. Riders sit on a spinning disk that is raised up a huge tower. The tower then topples over and bounces back up. All the while, it's looping around and around.

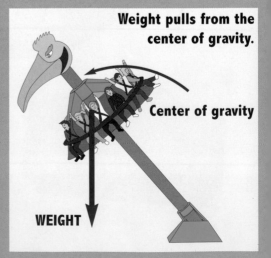

Weight pulls from the center of gravity.

Center of gravity

WEIGHT

DID YOU KNOW?

Your body's center of gravity is somewhere within your hips.

You may feel as if a ride could fall but it is carefully balanced.

CHAPTER 5: ENERGY

You are full of **energy.** In fact, everything in the universe has energy. Energy makes things work. Without it, nothing would happen.

WHAT IS ENERGY?

Energy comes in many different forms. Heat, light, sound, and motion are all forms of energy. A roller coaster gets its energy from motion. It also gives off energy in the form of sound and heat.

Burning fuel, such as wood, produces energy. This fire has both heat and light energy.

As a roller coaster roars and rumbles along a track, it produces sound energy.

MECHANICAL ENERGY

Anything that is in motion has **mechanical energy.** Many machin[es] have mechanical energy. A combination of moving parts enab[le] machines to do their work.

Mechanical energy comes from movement. It is a combination of **potential energy** and **kinetic ener[gy].** Potential energy is energy that a[n] object stores when it is still. Tha[t] energy becomes kinetic energy when an object starts to move.

On a roller coaster, energy is constantly changing from potent[ial] energy to kinetic energy and bac[k] again.

ANGING ENERGY

rgy often changes form, depending on what the energy is doing.

Anything that is hot has **heat energy.** Some of a roller coaster's kinetic energy becomes heat energy during the ride. That's because the wheels and other moving parts rub together during the ride. That rubbing creates **friction,** which in turn generates heat.

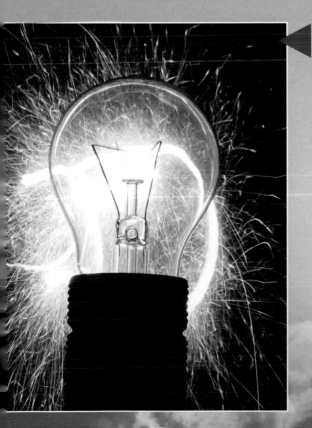

Light is **radiant energy.** Solar energy is another example of radiant energy. Lightbulbs give off radiant energy, but they are powered by **electrical energy**. Many machines need electricity to run. An electric motor is often used to start a roller coaster. During the ride, it is powered by kinetic energy.

Without the Sun's energy, there would be no life on Earth.

CHAPTER 6: KINETIC ENERGY

Kinetic energy is the energy of movement. Fast objects have lots of kinetic energy.

WHAT HAS KINETIC ENERGY?

Anything that moves has kinetic energy. An object with no kinetic energy is completely still. The faster an object moves the more kinetic energy it has.

Kinetic energy depends on both mass and speed. A heavier object in motion will have more kinetic energy than a lighter object. However, it is easier to make a light object move because it needs less kinetic energy.

At the bottom of a hill, the coaster has the most kinetic energy.

Fast speeds

The faster a roller coaster goes, the more kinetic energy it has.

STING ON ENERGY

...er coaster cars weigh several tons and hurtle
...ng at awesome speeds. Because of their large masses
...I high speeds, coaster cars have huge amounts of kinetic energy.

...oaster car gains kinetic energy as it speeds down a
... The pull of gravity accelerates the car
...aster and faster speeds.

THAT'S AMAZING!

A roller coaster can have as
much kinetic energy as a
thousand people running.

Potential energy is energy that is stored, waiting to be put to use. Objects positioned at a height store potential energy. When an object falls, its potential energy changes into kinetic energy. Roller coasters must store lots of potential energy to go fast.

POTENTIAL FOR SPEED

Roller coasters don't have motors. However, a mechanical device is used to pull roller coaster cars up the first hill. That builds up potential energy. The cars have the most potential energy at the top of the hill. The higher the hill, the more potential energy the cars will have.

When the cars roll downhill, gravity pulls the cars faster and faster. The potential energy changes into kinetic energy. As the cars climb the next hill, kinetic energy becomes potential energy once more.

STORING ENERGY

Hills on a roller coaster ride are designed to store potential energy. A strong motor tows the coaster up the first hill. At the top, the roller car has lots of potential energy. Larger hills store more potential energy, which provides the fastest rides.

At the top of the hill, the roller coaster has the most potential energy.

Speeds slow as kinetic energy decreases.

Height

The height of this roller coaster gives lots of potential energy.

DID YOU KNOW?

Potential energy is any type of stored energy. Stretched elastic bands and compressed springs also store potential energy.

Each time a roller coaster car climbs a hill or races down it, its energy changes from potential to kinetic and back again. Energy cannot be created or destroyed. It simply changes from one form to another. That is known as **conservation of energy.**

SWAPPING ENERGIES

You might wonder what happens to the kinetic energy of a moving car when the **brakes** are applied. Braking turns kinetic energy into heat energy, because the brakes rub against the cars to produce friction. Friction is a force that slows objects down. It is produced when two objects rub together. You feel the heat from friction when you rub your hands together. Car brakes get as hot as 600° F (315° C)!

Going up and down hills swaps potential energy with kinetic energy.

roller coaster's kinetic or
tential energy doesn't only
ove the cars. Some of it
comes heat or sound
ergy. Even so, the
ount of energy
ays the same. It
ly changes form.

DID YOU KNOW?

When most people talk about energy conservation, they mean saving energy by using less of it. Many people worry that Earth will run out of fossil fuels, such as oil and coal, which we now use to meet many of our energy needs.

HOW IT WORKS

This diagram shows how energy changes from one form to another during a roller coaster ride.

START

1. THE START

The ride starts with an electric motor pulling the coaster car up a huge hill. The motor's electrical energy becomes potential energy (stored energy).

2. FIRST DROP

As the coaster drops down the first hill it speeds up. The fall turns the initial potential energy into kinetic energy (energy from motion).

3. SECOND HILL

The coaster climbs up the next hill and slows almost to a stop. The kinetic energy has been turned back into potential energy.

5. BRAKE RUN
The ride ends with the coaster braking and coming to a stop. Braking creates friction, which turns the last remaining kinetic energy into heat energy.

4. LOOPS AND BENDS
Then, the coaster car travels the loops and turns of the ride. Its potential energy and kinetic energy keep swapping back and forth throughout the ride. However, the coaster also loses energy to friction.

GLOSSARY

Acceleration: a change in speed or direction; an object speeding up is said to accelerate

Airtime: the feeling of being weightless on a roller coaster

Brakes: devices that use friction to slow something down

Center of gravity: the point where an object's weight is concentrated

Conservation of energy: the principle that energy can never be created or destroyed, but only turned from one form into another

Deceleration: a decrease in speed or direction

Electrical energy: a type of energy that causes electricity to flow

Energy: the ability to make something happen

Forces: pushes or pulls that change the shape, speed, or direction of an object

Free fall: when an object drops with just the force of gravity

Friction: a force that resists movement. Rough surfaces cause friction.

G-force: a measure of force on your body from acceleration. One g is the same as the normal weight you feel from gravity.

Gravity: the force of attraction between objects. Gravity pulls objects toward Earth.

Heat energy: the energy in heat

Kinetic energy: a type of energy from movement

Mass: how much substance something contains. It causes an object to resist being accelerated.

Matter: anything that has mass that takes up space

Mechanical energy: the energy of motion that is used to perform work. Mechanical energy can be either potential energy or kinetic energy.

Potential energy: a type of energy that is stored

Radiant energy: energy that travels in electromagnetic waves. Light energy and solar energy are radiant energy.

Speed: how fast an object moves

Weight: the pull of gravity on an object's mass

Weightlessness: having little or no weight

INDEX